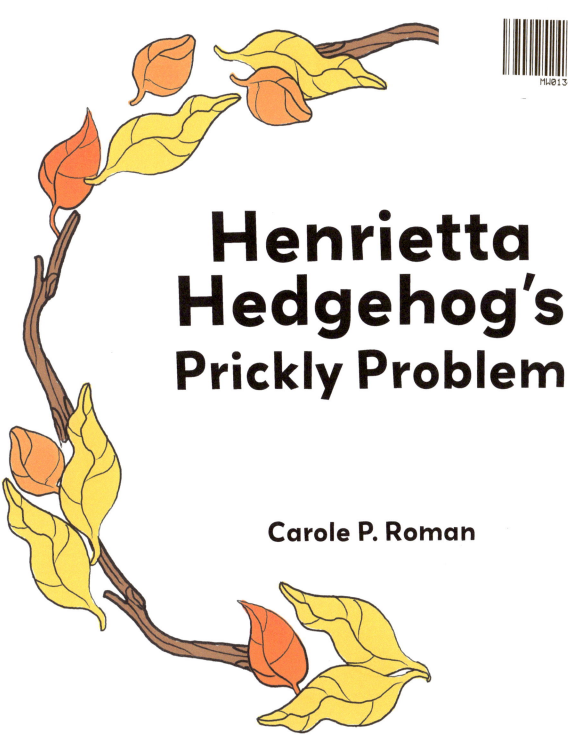

Henrietta Hedgehog's Prickly Problem

Carole P. Roman

Disclaimer

This is a work of fiction. Names, characters, business, events, locations and incidents are the products of the author's imagination. Any resemblance to actual persons, living or dead, or actual events is purely coincidental.

Hardcover ISBN: 979-8-218-07195-0

Paperback. ISBN: 978-1-950080-07-6

Chelshire, Inc.

For my daughters-in-law, Jennifer and Sharon, who taught me so much.

Always be a first-rate version of yourself, instead of a second-rate version of somebody else.

– Judy Garland

Henrietta Hedgehog rolled into a tight ball under her quilt. She didn't want to go to school today.

Mama Hedgehog stood in the doorway. "Henrietta, stop trying to hide! You'll be late."

"Mrs. Shrew will be mad if I am late," she said with a sniff. "I don't want to go to school." A big fat tear slid down her cheek.

"What happened? I thought you loved school!" Mama said.

"I do love school, Mama. It's just...just...I hate being a hedgehog."

"You hate being a hedgehog! That's... that's..." Mama sat on the edge of the bed. "Why?"

"The other kids make fun of me. They say my spines are scary!"

Mama Hedgehog wiped Henrietta's tears away. "They're not scary. You have beautiful quills."

Henrietta looked at herself in the mirror.

"I don't know about that, Mama. The kids won't sit close to me because they say they're very sharp. I wish I had a bushy tail like a squirrel or soft fur like a ferret. Anything but these pesky things," she sighed.

Henrietta waited for Mama to leave and then took a paper bag from under her pillow. She shoved it into her backpack.

After breakfast, Henrietta hurried to the hollowed-out log near the school. She looked around to make sure she was alone. Henrietta took out the bag from her backpack. Inside was a mask she had made with construction paper and a rubber band.

She slipped it over her head and covered her mouth with it. She looked at her reflection in a puddle and smiled. She looked like Bella Beaver.

Henrietta decided she looked very pretty, indeed.

She ran into the school just before the door closed and slid into her seat at her desk.

Bella Beaver did a double-take. Her brows lowered in hurt and anger. They had identical-looking mouths! Bella asked, "Are you making fun of me?"

Henrietta shook her head in disbelief. "Of course not. I wanted—"

"*Ha ha.*" Ryan Rabbit pointed to Henrietta. "Look at those goofy teeth!"

Henrietta heard laughter in the back of the room.

Mrs. Shrew glared at Henrietta and ordered, "Take those off!"

Henrietta removed them and stuffed them into her backpack. Bella was still looking hurt.

During recess, all the students followed her out. Woodpeckers and moles, mice and foxes all surrounded Henrietta in the school yard.

"Why'd you put on fake choppers?" Wendy Woodpecker demanded.

"So you'd have fangs to match the pointy quills?" Maxwell Mole asked.

Shelby Snake slithered around her, snickering. "You looked twice as *ssssilly*," she hissed.

"That wasn't very nice to make fun of my teeth," Bella said.

"I wasn't making fun of you. I wanted to look like you." Henrietta lowered her eyes. "Maybe the kids would like me more if I looked like a beaver."

Bella shook her head. "They tease me about my teeth all the time." She paused and reached out to touch Henrietta's coat but stopped.

"I wish I had your sharp quills to protect me," Bella said wistfully.

"Oh, these old things?" Henrietta straightened her quills out. "I wish I had fur like... like... like..."

"Me?" Frannie Ferret shook herself from under some leaves where she was hiding. "I may have a pretty coat, but ferret means 'little thief.' Just think what the other kids have to say about that!"

Henrietta pursed her tiny mouth. She still wasn't convinced. "You have no idea how hard it is to be a hedgehog."

They heard a scabbling of feet behind them.

"Sometimes they pick on me. They call me Squeaky," Spencer Squirrel's voice piped up as he jumped off the side of a tree. "They complain that even my nails make too much noise."

"Look at my legs." Wally Weasel waddled to where they were sitting. "My legs are short, and I can't do anything about it, " he wailed.

"I think you're cute." Bella batted her eyelashes at him.

Wally ignored her and kept talking, his eyes large and sorrowful. "They call me names all the time. No matter how big my body gets, I can't make my legs longer."

"I wish I could snap my fingers and change my appearance," Henrietta said.

"When I complain, my mom says that there is nothing wrong with the way I look." Dylan Deer approached them, her graceful legs delicately picking her way through the grass. She shook her head. "She told me that our differences make us interesting as well as beautiful!"

"That's easy for you to say. Look at you," Henrietta said.

Dylan sighed. "Well, I hated my freckles. The other kids called me Dotty. I learned every deer has different marks on their bodies that show our individuality. Really, Henrietta, what would you be without your quills?"

"I could change my teeth, but then I wouldn't be a busy beaver, would I?" Bella said.

Soon, Henrietta was surrounded by a cluster of critters. She looked at each one. Ferrets had small legs so they could burrow underground; beavers needed large teeth to chew wood, and hedgehogs had quills... She glanced at her quills and considered them.

"Your quills are part of you. They are important for your protection. If people don't accept you because of how you look--" Dylan told her.

"Or sound," said Spencer.

"Or walk," Wally added.

"Who needs them!" Henrietta burst out. Everyone laughed.

Henrietta looked around the clearing with a start. She counted several new faces. They didn't seem to care about her quills.

At the end of the school day, Bella reached out to take Henrietta's hand.

"Come on, let's walk home together."

Henrietta walked carefully, making sure not to poke Bella with her quill.

Bella smiled back, showing all her teeth. "Just be yourself, Henrietta. You are perfect just the way you are."

About the Author

Carole P. Roman is the award-winning author of over fifty children's books. Whether it's pirates, princesses, spies, or discovering the world around us, her books have enchanted educators, parents, and her diverse audience of children of all ages. Writing is her passion and one of her favorite pastimes. Roman reinvents herself frequently, and her family calls her the "mother of reinvention." She resides on Long Island, near her children and grandchildren.

About the Illustrator

Mateya Arkova is a freelance children's book illustrator, based in Sofia, Bulgaria. Being a children's book illustrator is her dream job; in the past ten years, she created more then 50 titles with talented authors from around the world.

She works with Bulgarian and foreign publishing houses; many of the books are translated for the French, Chinese, and American book markets.

Mateya is drawing mainly in traditional methods as watercolour and pencil. Her style conveys is conveying elegant movements in the illustration scenes and pastel colour palettes. She is inspired by walks in the wild nature with her dog, kayaking, and listening to music.

Her series includes:

Captain No Beard

If You Were Me and Lived in- Cultural

If You Were Me and Lived in- Historical

Bedtime Nursery series

Oh Susannah series- Early Reader and coloring book

Mindfulness for Kids
with co-author J. Robin Albertson-Wren

The Big Book of Silly Jokes for Kids; 800 plus Jokes! 1 and 2

Spies, Code Talkers, and Secret Agents
A World War 2 Book for Kids

Grady Whill and the Templeton Codex:
A Superhero High School Adventure

Giggles Galore

Mrs.Rabbit's Friendsgiving Dinner

CPSIA information can be obtained
at www.ICGtesting.com
Printed in the USA
BVHW010223160223
658526BV00002B/6